NUTS
A Cookbook

NUTS

A Cookbook

CHARTWELL
BOOKS, INC.

A QUANTUM BOOK

Published by Chartwell Books
A Division of Book Sales Inc
114 Northfield Avenue
Edison, New Jersey 08837
USA

ISBN 0-7858-0789-6

QUMNAC

This book was produced by
Quantum Books Ltd
6 Blundell Street
London N7 9BH

Printed in Singapore by Star Standard Industries Pte Ltd

In memory of
Richard D. Taleff,
whose love of coconut was inspirational.

ACKNOWLEDGMENTS

Special thanks to Steve Smith, without whom this book would still be just an idea. Thanks to my family for their support and to all my friends who served as willing guinea pigs for these recipes, particularly Martie LeBare, Michael McEvoy, Beth and Fred Rust, Alan and Jeanette Mittelsdorf, John Morse, my sisters Joan Rogers and Lynn Stillman and special thanks to my mother, Ann Rogers, for the dog nutcracker.

Thanks also to Carla Glasser and everyone at the Nolan-Lehr Group. Special thanks to Sidney Miner and Clare Wellnitz, and to Marta Hallett, Ellen Milionis, Jill Hamilton, Tom Fiffer, Rose K. Phillips, Linda Winters, and everyone else at Running Heads. Last but not least, thanks to Dexter Samuel for all his help.

We would like to thank the following people for their support during this project: the Jacobson and Ehlers families, Judy Devine for her love and inspiration, and Maggie Jones.

Thanks also to Jill Bock, Michele Cohen, Beth Farb, Kim Kelling, Tina KIem, Linda Winters and everyone at Jenkins & Page and 2B.

Our special thanks to those companies who generously loaned us their beautiful wares: Ceramica, Jim Mellgren at Dean & DeLuca, Platypus, Pottery Barn and Pauline Kelly at Zona.

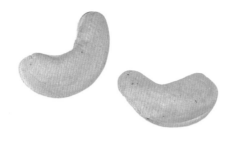

THREE
MAIN COURSES

FIVE
DESSERTS

RECIPE LIST

RECIPE LIST BY NUT

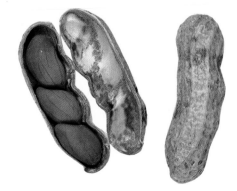

INTRODUCTION

Nuts are seeds or fruits consisting of soft edible hearts in hard or woody shells. Popular long before scientists discovered their nutritional value, nuts were a staple in the diet of early hunter-gatherers, and archeologists have found traces of them in prehistoric campfires. These countless ages of nut consumption can be attributed only to one thing – nuts are delicious.

We now know that besides tasting so good, nuts are an excellent source of protein as well as the B vitamins, vitamin E and minerals such as iron, calcium, magnesium and potassium. Nuts do have a high fat content, but much of this fat is polyunsaturated or monounsaturated, so eating nuts does not generally increase blood cholesterol. One exception is the coconut, which has a relatively high saturated fat level but seems, in light of its unique taste, worth an occasional indulgence.

Because fat spoils faster than starch or protein, nuts tend to become rancid if stored too long. Unshelled nuts will keep in a cool, dry place for several months, while shelled nuts, if refrigerated in airtight containers, will keep for only one or two months, depending on their fat content. All nuts freeze well and will keep in the freezer for about six months.

When buying nuts in the shell, make sure they feel heavy for their size and do not rattle much. Look for nuts of uniform color, without cracks or holes that will cause them to spoil faster.

Roasting brings out the full flavor of nuts, and most cultures serve roasted nuts solo – plain or salted. Some cuisines, particularly Middle Eastern and African ones, are more adventurous and use ground nuts as thickening agents, while Europeans and Americans tend to relegate them to snacks and delectable desserts. But nuts are much more versatile than these limited uses suggest. This book will crack open the many diverse and delicious ways of using nuts in cooking. The recipes feature the twelve most readily available and useful nuts and a brief description of each follows.

ALMONDS

Botanically, the almond is not a true nut but a stone fruit, like peaches or apricots. Almonds probably originated in the Near East, but they have long been cultivated throughout the tropics. Revered by the Romans, almonds were once regarded so highly that people believed dreaming about them would bring good luck. They came to America with Spanish missionaries en route to California – still the major American supplier – and they remain the dominant nut in world trade and the most widely grown and eaten tree nut. Where they are cultivated their blossoms serve as a fragrant herald of spring. Almonds come in two types – bitter and sweet. Bitter almonds contain prussic acid, a poison that must be leached by heating, and they are used almost exclusively for almond oils and extracts. Sweet almonds are the familiar ones used for eating and in cooking. Almonds are rich in protein, calcium and riboflavin, and most of their fat is monounsaturated. Their saturated fat content is among the lowest of all nuts.

BRAZIL NUTS

Brazil nuts, as their name indicates, originated in the tropical rain forests of South America, and they are a truly wild food. Attempts to cultivate them have met with resounding failure, and virtually all of the Brazil nuts on the market come from wild trees. They grow clustered together like orange segments, in coconut-type shells roughly the size of an adult man's head that weigh up to five pounds. Each shell contains twelve to twenty-four nuts and is harvested from November until June by laborers called *caboclo*, who gather them from the ground after they have fallen from towering 100- to 150-foot high trees. It is not a good idea to seek shelter under a Brazil nut tree during rainstorms or high winds! After harvesting the nuts, the *caboclo* take them to trading posts where they are shelled manually. Given the highly labor-intensive method of gathering Brazil nuts – and the fact that they are 65 per cent oil and have a very short shelf life – their price is relatively reasonable. Although their fat content is one of the highest and they contain more saturated fat than most nuts, Brazil nuts are still a good source of vitamin A, the B vitamins and some minerals. Only pecans and walnuts have greater nutritional value.

CASHEWS

The cashew is an evergreen shrub native to the West Indies, Brazil and India. Today's leading cashew exporters are Mozambique and Tanzania, where Portuguese colonists took cashews and planted them. Related to the mango and the pistachio, the cashew grows hanging below a mango-like, pear-shaped edible fruit called the cashew apple. Because the cashew apple spoils within twenty-four hours of harvest, it is almost never exported, and the fortunate few who have tried this fruit say it is even tastier than the cashew nut. Cashew nuts are always sold shelled, because the cardol layer between the shell and the nut is caustic and will blister the skin on contact. The cardol is removed by heating the nuts, and the caustic liquid rendered in the process is used in more than 250 medicines, resins and industrial products. Cashews are about 48 per cent fat – almost all of it nonsaturated or monounsaturated – and they provide vitamin A, some B vitamins, iron and calcium.

CHESTNUTS

The chestnut tree is native to southern Europe and has been exported as much for its timber as for its nuts, which grow in groups of two or three in a prickly green husk. One variety grows one nut to a husk and is called a marron. Because chestnuts contain so much starch and so little oil, they are the only nut treated as a vegetable and must be boiled or roasted before eating. Further, they are sweet and soft, without the characteristic crunchiness of nuts. Low in protein and fat, but high in carbohydrates, chestnuts provide some B vitamins, vitamin E and potassium. Chestnuts will keep fresh at room temperature for only a short time, but if they are refrigerated, they will keep for two to three months.

COCONUTS

The coconut's origin is unknown, because the oceans seem to have carried it to tropical beaches all over the world. Coconut palms bear fruit throughout the year, and coconuts are a staple crop in many parts of the world. The Philippines and Indonesia are the world's chief coconut exporters. Most cultures use every part of the nut in some way: the husk woven into rope and mats; the shells formed into utensils and vessels; the flesh eaten fresh or dried to make copra – an oil used extensively in cosmetics and margarines. Even the sap is fermented to make a drink. Coconuts taste best when picked young, with greenish white skins and flesh tender enough to be eaten with a spoon. Unfortunately, they are rarely available this way, except where they grow. In the supermarket a "fresh" coconut should feel heavy, and you should be able to hear the liquid sloshing around inside. (If not, the nut has dried out.) Its three "eyes" should be dry, without any mold or rancid smell. If it smells sour throw it away! Coconuts contain a lot of fat, which, unlike the fat in other nuts, is almost all saturated.

They also contain some B vitamins and minerals. Due to its high fat content, coconut flesh spoils quickly once the nut is cracked. Fresh flesh can be refrigerated for one week or frozen for several months. Dried flakes can be refrigerated or frozen for several months.

HAZELNUTS

Chinese lore says the hazelnut is one of the five sacred nourishments bestowed on humans, and hazelnuts have been cultivated continuously in China for 4,500 years. Members of the birch family, hazelnuts grow in clusters, partially covered by a green skin. Many species grow wild in temperate areas, but only three are cultivated as a cash crop: the Turkish hazel, the Mediterranean filbert, and the Old World cobnut. The hazel is a little smaller than the other two, but once the nuts are shelled it is difficult to distinguish them. Only the cobnut is grown in North America. The main exporters of hazelnuts are Mediterranean countries, with Turkey being the largest producer in the world and Germany and England ranking first and second, respectively, in consumption. They are rich in some of the B vitamins as well as C and E, and they are a good source of protein. They will keep for many months in a cool place and up to two years in the refrigerator.

MACADAMIAS

Macadamias are also called Queensland nuts, because they originated in the forests of Queensland in northeastern Australia. Many Australian macadamia trees are 100 to 150 years old. They are the only indigenous Australian plant ever developed into a cash crop. They are cultivated on a large scale, however, only in Hawaii, where they have thrived in the rich volcanic soil since being introduced in 1882. Macadamias were supposedly named by Australia's foremost botanist, Baron Ferdinand Van Mueller, in 1857, for his friend Dr John MacAdam, who never saw or ate one. Macadamias are harvested when they fall from their trees. Given their hard shells and tendency to mildew in the shell, they are almost always sold shelled – raw or roasted. Because their high oil content makes them spoil rapidly they are usually sold in vacuum-packed jars. Once the container is opened, the nuts should be consumed quickly, which is usually not a problem.

PEANUTS

Not really a nut, but rather a legume or pea, the peanut originated in South America, in the tropical lower Andes of Bolivia. Today peanuts are grown in every subtropical region on earth, thanks to the intervention of humans. The world's largest growers are China and India, but their production is consumed domestically mostly in the form of oil. Nigeria, where the Portuguese introduced the nut, is todays largest exporter. The two types of peanut, Spanish and Virginia, both grow underground, encased in fibrous shells. (Peanuts have also been known as groundnuts or monkeynuts.) Virginia peanuts are a bit longer and have a stronger taste but are otherwise indistinguishable from Spanish.

Both varieties are highly nutritious, with approximately 25 per cent protein as well as some of the B vitamins, vitamin E and minerals such as phosphorus and iron. Peanuts are also high in unsaturated fat, and peanut oil's high smoking point permits frying at high temperatures without burning. Unshelled, peanuts will keep for several months in a cool, dry place. Shelled, they will keep for two months in a cool place – longer in the refrigerator.

PECANS

This former staple food of the indigenous peoples of North America is the only truly "All-American" nut. A species of hickory, the pecan grows wild on tall trees in the temperate zones. Wild pecans tend to be smaller than cultivated ones and have a lower percentage of kernel and more shell. Pecans are harvested by shaking the trees, causing the nuts to fall to the ground. They are slightly less fatty than their relative the walnut, but their 70 per cent oil content – 95 per cent of it unsaturated – causes them to turn rancid soon after shelling.

Pecans are rich in several useful minerals and some B vitamins, and they are an excellent source of B6, which is present almost exclusively in foods that require cooking, which destroys this vitamin. Unshelled pecans will keep in a cool place for a few months. Shelled pecans, stored in an airtight container, will last for a few weeks in the refrigerator.

PINE NUTS

Also known as pine kernels, pignolias and Indian nuts, the nuts of many pine trees are edible and have been used in cuisines the world over for centuries. Only the nuts of the stone pine, however, which grows wild from Portugal to the Black Sea, are cultivated globally as a cash crop. Pine nuts have a soft shell and no skin, and all commercially available types are sold shelled. Some varieties, such as the piñon of the southwestern United States, are available only locally. Although expensive, pine nuts have a strong resinous flavor that allows cooks to use fewer of them than other milder nuts. This flavour mellows when the nuts are roasted. Pine nuts spoil quickly and should always be refrigerated in an airtight container where they will last for a few weeks.

PISTACHIOS

Pistachios are native to central and western Asia and were brought to Rome from Syria in the first century. The Mongol emperors referred to pistachios as the nuts of paradise, but their new European admirers called them green almonds. Today the pistachio tree, a ten-foot-tall deciduous species of turpentine tree, thrives in the poor rocky soil of the Mediterranean, the Middle East and the southwestern U.S. The nuts are encased in a gummy husk, which is removed by soaking. As the nuts dry, the shells gape open and take on their familiar appearance. Pistachio shells are naturally tan; red pistachios have been dyed and should be avoided.

WALNUTS

Walnuts are native to the temperate zones of Europe and Asia and were introduced long ago to similar climates all over the world. Their well-preserved remains have even been found in Pompeii. Walnut trees have long been considered an excellent source of timber, and walnuts were once believed to ward off disease and increase fertility (inspiring the custom of scattering them at weddings in some cultures the way others use rice). Walnuts come in two varieties: the European, also called the English or Persian; and the black. The European variety of which France is the leading producer became known as English walnuts because the English had a thriving trade in them in centuries past. But as with almonds, Spanish missionaries introduced them to North America via California. Because black walnuts are hard to crack, with sticky shells, they have resisted commercial exploitation. Some consider them less tasty than European walnuts, but this has not prevented their use in desserts and ice cream. The husks and casings of European walnuts are used to make a liqueur known in Europe as brou. Walnuts have a high fat content, most of it unsaturated, and they should be kept refrigerated in an airtight container once shelled.

SHELLING, PEELING, TOASTING AND ROASTING

ALMONDS

To shell: Cover with boiling water and soak for 15 to 20 minutes. Drain and cool. Crack with a nutcracker.

To peel (or blanch): Drop into boiling water, boil for 1 minute, then drain and rinse in cold water. Pinch one end of the skin, and the nut will pop out the other end. Watch out for flying almonds!

To toast: Heat 1 tablespoon butter or oil for each cup of nuts in a skillet large enough to hold the nuts in one layer. Sauté over medium-low heat, tossing frequently to prevent burning, until golden brown, 15 to 30 minutes. Almonds can also be deep-fried.

To roast: Preheat the oven to 350º. Place the almonds in a single layer in a shallow pan and roast, stirring often, until golden brown, about 30 to 45 minutes. The almonds will continue to cook after being removed from the oven, so be sure to take them out just before the desired degree of doneness.

BRAZIL NUTS

To shell: Drop into boiling water and boil gently for 3 minutes. Drain and cool. Crack with a nutcracker or preheat the oven to 400º and roast in the shell in a shallow pan in a single layer for about 20 minutes. Then cool, crack and shell. To peel: Drop into boiling water with 1^1/$_2$ teaspoons baking soda for each quart of water. Simmer for 2 minutes, slip off the skins while the nuts are still warm. To toast: Heat 1 tablespoon butter or oil per cup of nuts in a skillet large enough to hold the nuts in one layer. Sauté over medium heat for 5 to 10 minutes for whole nuts or 2 to 3 minutes for sliced nuts, stirring often, until golden brown.

To roast: Follow the instructions for roasting almonds, but decrease the time to 20 to 30 minutes, or roast in the shell as previously described.

To slice: Cover with cold water in a saucepan. Bring slowly to a boil, lower the heat and simmer for 2 to 3 minutes. This makes it possible to slice the nuts without breaking them.

CASHEWS

Cashews are always sold shelled and peeled.

To toast: Follow the instructions for toasting almonds.

To roast: Follow the instructions for roasting almonds, but decrease the roasting time to 10 to 20 minutes.

To shell and peal: Preheat the oven to 400°. Cut an X on the flat side of each chestnut. Roast in a shallow pan in a single layer for about 20 minutes or until the chestnuts feel soft. Shell and peel the chestnuts as soon as they are cool enough to handle. (Expect to burn your fingers slightly). Use a sharp knife to get the shelling started. Pull off the shell and as much of the skin as possible. Chestnuts with stubborn skins can be reheated, either in water or in the oven, or even in oil in a skillet. Try peeling again, gently squeezing the chestnut or even breaking it apart if necessary.

You can also "cheat" and buy the imported French brands of chestnuts that come vacuum-packed or packed in water. They are delicious and can save you a lot of time.

HAZELNUTS

To shell: Crack with a nutcracker. To roast and peel: Preheat the oven to 350°. Spread the nuts in a single layer on a baking tray or in a shallow tin. Dry the nuts in the oven for about 15 minutes or until the skins begin to flake and the nuts appear light brown. Remove from the oven and wrap in a piece of kitchen paper. Place the kitchen paper in a plastic bag until the nuts are cool enough to handle. Rub the hazelnuts together in the kitchen paper rubbing off as much of the brown skin as possible. The hazelnuts are now roasted and peeled. Alternatively, put them under the broiler for a few minutes until the skins flake. Then proceed as directed.

MACADAMIAS

Virtually all macadamia nuts are sold shelled. Some are already roasted and salted, so be sure to check the label.

To roast: Follow the instructions for roasting almonds, but reduce the time to 12 to 15 minutes.

PEANUTS

To shell and peel: You can usually shell and peel peanuts by hand, either before or after roasting. If removing the brown skins proves difficult, cover the shelled peanuts with boiling water and set aside for 5 minutes. Drain. The skins should then slide off quite easily but the nuts must then dry for several hours or for several minutes in the oven.

To roast: Follow the instructions for roasting almonds. Shelled peanuts should roast to a nice golden brown in 15 to 20 minutes. In the shell, roast them for about 25 minutes.

To toast: Peanuts are usually toasted by deep frying but may be toasted as almonds, reducing the time to 8 to 10 minutes. To deep-fry: heat enough oil to cover the peanuts to 350º. As when roasting, these nuts will continue to cook after being removed from the oil, so stop toasting just before they are done to your satisfaction.

COCONUTS

One coconut weighing approximately 1¹/₂ pounds yields about 4 cups flesh.

To shell and peel: Preheat the oven to 400º. Poke holes in the 3 coconut eyes with an ice pick or other sharp object. Drain the liquid (this is not coconut milk) and taste a few drops. If it tastes at all sour, discard the coconut and try another one. Discard the liquid unless the flesh is to be frozen. Place the coconut in the oven for 20 minutes, then let it cool slightly. Holding it over a large howl, strike it all the way around the center with the back edge of a large, heavy knife or cleaver until it splits. Pry the heavy shell off with a screwdriver and remove the thin brown skin with a vegetable peeler. Wash and dry the coconut flesh, then grate or shred according to the recipe.

To save time with little loss of taste, buy frozen grated unsweetened coconut – available in ethnic markets or specialty stores. To freeze your own coconut either in chunks or grated, strain the reserved liquid from the center and combine it with the flesh in an airtight container. To toast: Preheat the oven to 350º. Spread freshly grated or shredded coconut in a shallow pan and toast for 5 to 10 minutes, or until golden brown. Stir occasionally to toast evenly. Cool on paper towels. For faster but less even toasting, spread in a shallow pan and place 3 to 4 inches under the broiler for 3 to 6 minutes, or until golden brown. Stir often and watch carefully to make sure it does not burn. To make coconut milk from fresh coconut: Shell and peel the coconut as directed. When all of the flesh is washed and dried, cut it into 1-inch or smaller squares and put half of them into the bowl of a blender or food processor fitted with a steel blade. Bring 3 cups water or milk – or a combination – almost to a boil. Pour half of it into the blender with the coconut flesh and process as finely as possible. Line a bowl with a double thickness of cheesecloth and pour the processed mixture into it. Repeat with the second half of the flesh and liquid. Pick up the edges of the cheesecloth and raise it slowly allowing the liquid to drain out. Squeeze the cheesecloth gently to extract the remaining liquid but not the pulp. This should yield about 3 cups. Seal in an airtight container. The milk will keep for 2 to 3 days in the refrigerator or several months in the freezer.

Dried coconut, which will keep indefinitely in an airtight container, works well when preparing coconut milk. Proceed as for fresh coconut, using 3 to 4 cups dried coconut and an equal amount of liquid. Good canned coconut milks are available at Asian and specialist markets. If you buy sweetened coconut milk, you will have to compensate accordingly in the recipes.

ONE
APPETIZERS
AND SOUPS

Chicken Liver and Pistachio Paté

3/4 cup unsalted butter

1 pound chicken livers, washed and drained

1/2 cup chopped celery ribs and tops from the celery heart

1 cup chopped mushrooms

1/2 cup chopped onion

1 garlic clove, chopped

1/4 cup cognac or brandy

1/4 teaspoon cayenne pepper

2 teaspoons dry mustard

1/4 teaspoon freshly grated nutmeg

1/2 teaspoon dried thyme, crushed

1/4 teaspoon ground allspice

1/2 teaspoon salt

1/2 teaspoon freshly ground black pepper

1 cup shelled, peeled, dried and roasted pistachios

Serves 12 to 16

Preparation time: 30 minutes, plus 4 hours to set and 30 minutes to come to room temperature

Preheat the oven to 300º.

In a large skillet over medium-high heat, melt 1/4 cup of the butter and add the chicken livers, celery, mushrooms, onion and garlic. Cook for 3 to 5 minutes or until the livers have begun to brown lightly but are still pink inside. Add the cognac or brandy, cover, lower the heat and simmer for 5 more minutes.

Remove from the heat and place the contents in the bowl of a blender or food processor fitted with a steel blade. Add the spices and the remaining butter, cut into chunks, and process until smooth. (While processing the mixture, stop several times to scrape down the sides of the bowl.)

Fold the nuts, reserving a few for garnish, into the processed liver mixture by hand. Pour the mixture into a 3- or 4-cup crock, bowl, mold or terrine and refrigerate for 4 hours or overnight, until firm.

Serve in the crock or bowl or unmold onto a plate by dipping the container into hot water for a few moments, covering it with the plate and inverting. Garnish with the reserved pistachios, whole or chopped.

Allow the pâté to stand at room temperature for 30 minutes before serving.

COLD NOODLES WITH SPICY ALMOND SAUCE

$^1/_4$ cup vegetable oil

1 cup slivered blanched almonds

2 tablespoons soy sauce

3 tablespoons white rice vinegar (white wine vinegar may be substituted)

1 teaspoon sugar

1 tablespoon grated fresh ginger

2 garlic cloves, crushed

2 tablespoons dry sherry

2-3 tablespoons hot chili oil (to taste)

1 pound soba noodles or spaghetti

3 scallions, thinly sliced diagonally

1 7-inch cucumber, peeled, seeded and cut into matchsticks

In a 10-inch skillet over medium-high heat, heat 3 tablespoons of the vegetable oil. Add the almonds and fry until brown, about 2 minutes. Remove about $^1/_3$ of the almonds with a slotted spoon and drain them on a paper towel. Reserve.

Put the remaining almonds and the oil into the bowl of a blender or food processor fitted with a steel blade. Process, pulsing on and off, until a smooth "butter" forms.

Add the next 7 ingredients to the food processor and continue to process until the mixture is smooth and well combined. (The mixture may be made up to several days in advance to this point, refrigerated and brought to room temperature before serving.)

Cook the noodles until *al dente* according to package directions. Drain and rinse under cold water until they are thoroughly cooled. Drain again. Toss the noodles with the remaining tablespoon of oil and serve on a platter or individual plates, topped with the sauce and garnished with the scallions, cucumber and reserved almonds.

Serves 6

Preparation time: 30 minutes

FRESH FIGS WITH BLACK PEPPER AND HAZELNUTS

3/4 cup shelled, roasted and peeled hazelnuts

1 tablespoon hazelnut oil (vegetable oil may be substituted)

8 ripe fresh figs

2 teaspoons freshly cracked black pepper

Serves 4

Preparation time: 10 minutes

Place the hazelnuts in the bowl of a blender or food processor fitted with a steel blade. Grind the nuts, pulsing on and off a couple of times, until the ground nuts begin to stick together. Add the oil and continue to grind until a crunchy nut butter has formed.

Cut the figs in half lengthwise. Place a dollop of approximately 1/2 tablespoon nut butter in the cavity of each half and sprinkle with 1/8 teaspoon pepper.

Serve on individual appetizer plates or on a single large plate as part of an hors d'oeuvre table.

CHEDDAR, BEER AND PECAN CHEESECAKE

3 tablespoons unsalted butter

2^1/$_2$ cups roasted pecan pieces or halves

6 tablespoons unbleached all-purpose flour

^{1}/$_3$ teaspoon freshly ground white pepper

^{1}/$_2$ teaspoon cayenne pepper

1 teaspoon dry mustard

2 teaspoons Worcestershire sauce

^{1}/$_2$ cup beer or ale

1 pound sharp cheddar cheese, finely shredded

1 pound cream cheese at room temperature

4 large eggs at room temperature

Serves 16 as an appetizer, 8 as an entree

Preparation time: 2 hours, plus overnight to chill and 2 to 3 hours to come to room temperature

Preheat the oven to 350º.

Melt the butter and set it aside.

Generously grease an 8-inch springform pan. Set the pan in the center of a 12-inch square of aluminum foil and fold the foil up the sides of the pan, pressing it firmly against them.

In a blender or food processor fitted with a steel blade, process 1^1/$_2$ cups of the roasted pecans with 3 tablespoons of the flour, pulsing on and off, until the mixture resembles bread crumbs. Place the mixture in a small bowl and add the melted butter, mixing well. Firmly press the mixture into the bottom and halfway up the sides of the springform pan. Put the pan in the oven and bake for 10 minutes. Remove and cool to room temperature.

While the crust is baking, coarsely chop the remaining nuts and set aside. Then combine the white pepper, cayenne pepper, dry mustard and Worcestershire sauce in a 1-quart saucepan and whisk to remove any lumps. Add the beer or ale and whisk to combine. Heat over medium heat until the beer is hot and steaming. Remove from the heat. Add the cheddar cheese and whisk until smooth. (The mixture will look somewhat grainy. It should be only slightly warm to the touch. If not, let it cool slightly.)

In a large mixing bowl, beat the cream cheese until fluffy. Beat in the cheddar mixture and the remaining 3 tablespoons flour, until combined. Add the eggs one at a time, blending well after each addition. Fold in the remaining nuts.

Pour the mixture into the cooled crust. Bake for 40 minutes. Turn off the heat and let the cheesecake sit undisturbed in the oven for an additional 40 minutes.

Remove the cake from the oven, cool completely, then refrigerate overnight.

Remove the cake from the refrigerator a few hours before serving and allow to come to room temperature. Carefully release the spring and remove the sides of the pan. Slice and serve with cornichons and pickled onions if desired, or place on an hors d'oeuvre table.

FRIED WALNUT POLENTA WITH GORGONZOLA SAUCE

Polenta:

4 tablespoons unsalted butter

3 cups milk

$1/2$ teaspoon salt

1 cup stone-ground yellow cornmeal

1 cup chopped walnuts

Sauce:

$1^1/2$ cups milk

2 tablespoons unsalted butter

1 tablespoon minced shallot

3 tablespoons unbleached all-purpose flour

$1/3$ cup crumbled Gorgonzola cheese

salt and freshly ground black pepper to taste

parsley leaves for garnish (optional)

Serves 8

Preparation time: 1 hour, plus 2 hours or overnight to chill

Make the polenta. (This can be done a day ahead or earlier in the day.) Butter an $8^1/2$- x $4^1/2$-inch loaf pan or a $1^1/2$-quart mold with 1 tablespoon of the butter.

In a heavy saucepan over medium-high heat, combine the milk, salt, and another tablespoon of the butter. Heat to a simmer. While whisking constantly add the cornmeal in a trickle. When all the cornmeal has been added, lower the heat, maintaining a simmer, and cook, stirring constantly with a wooden spoon, until the mixture is thick enough to pull away from the sides of the pan, about 25 to 30 minutes. Stir in the chopped walnuts until well distributed. Pour immediately into the prepared pan. Cool, then cover and refrigerate for at least 2 hours or overnight.

Unmold the polenta by inverting the pan onto a board or plate and rubbing the pan with a towel dipped in hot water and wrung out. With a sharp knife, slice the unmolded polenta into $1/2$-inch-thick slices.

To make the sauce, scald the milk in a small saucepan. (Heat it until bubbles form around the edge of the pan.) Remove from the heat.

In another small saucepan, melt 2 tablespoons of butter over medium-high heat, add the shallot and sauté until it begins to look translucent, about 3 to 4 minutes. Add the flour and whisk constantly until bubbling but not browned, another 2 to 3 minutes. Whisk in the milk, stirring until smooth. Add the cheese and the salt and pepper to taste. Whisk until smooth. Lower the heat to low and simmer until thick, about 10 minutes. Meanwhile, in a large skillet, melt the remaining 2 tablespoons of butter over medium-high heat and sauté the polenta slices in batches, turning them over once, until golden brown on both sides. Serve hot, 2 slices per serving, with the sauce as well as parsley leaves for garnish if desired.

GINGERED CHESTNUT SOUP

2 tablespoons unsalted butter

1 large onion, chopped

$^1/_2$ pound carrots, scraped and chopped (about 3 or 4 carrots)

$^1/_4$ cup chopped fresh ginger

1 pound chestnuts, roasted, shelled and peeled

1 bay leaf

salt and freshly ground white pepper to taste

1 quart chicken broth

1 cup dry white wine

2 tablespoons fresh lemon juice

Serves 6

Preparation time: 1 hour 15 minutes

Melt the butter in a large saucepan over medium heat. Add the onion, carrots and ginger and sauté gently for 10 minutes.

Add the chestnuts, bay leaf, salt and white pepper, and broth. Bring the mixture to a boil, then cover. Lower the heat and simmer for 45 minutes. Remove the bay leaf and purée the mixture in batches in a blender or food processor fitted with a steel blade. Add the wine and lemon juice. (The soup can be prepared in advance to this point and refrigerated.)

Rinse the pan thoroughly, return the puréed soup to it and heat slowly stirring frequently to prevent sticking. You may add more broth if the soup is too thick for your taste, but remember that it will thin a little as it heats.

Serve garnished with a dollop of cream.

COCONUT-PRAWN SOUP

4¹/₂ cups coconut milk, made from 2 fresh coconuts (canned unsweetened coconut milk may be substituted)

2 medium-size onions, chopped

1 garlic clove, mashed

10 black peppercorns

3 coriander seeds

zest of 1 lemon, removed with a vegetable peeler or sharp knife

1 teaspoon cumin seeds

3 parsley sprigs

1 or 2 hot fresh chilies (to taste), seeded and coarsely chopped

1 pound raw shrimp, shelled, deveined and chopped

1 teaspoon sugar

2 tablespoons fresh lemon juice

salt to taste

4-6 peeled cooked shrimp for garnish (optional)

¹/₄ cup shredded fresh coconut for garnish (optional)

Serves 4 to 6

Preparation time: 2 hours

Place the coconut milk and onions in a medium-size saucepan and bring to a boil. Place the garlic, peppercorns, coriander seeds, lemon zest, cumin seeds, parsley and chilies in a spice bag or a piece of cheesecloth, tied shut, and add it to the saucepan. Cover, lower the heat and simmer for 25 minutes.

Add the shrimp, sugar, lemon juice and salt to taste and simmer for 5 minutes more. Remove the spice bag. Serve hot, garnished with whole shrimp and shredded coconut if desired.

CRANBERRY-ALMOND SOUP

1 cup blanched almonds

³/₄ cup granulated sugar

3¹/₂ cups water

1 3-inch cinnamon stick

3 cups cranberries

1 cup rosé wine

Serves 6 to 8

Preparation time: 30 minutes

Place the almonds and half the sugar in a blender or food processor fitted with a steel blade. Grind the mixture to a paste. Add ¹/₂ cup of the water and process again until the paste is very smooth. Set aside.

In a medium-size saucepan, bring the remaining 3 cups water to a boil. Add the remaining sugar and the cinnamon stick and stir to dissolve the sugar. Add the cranberries and the almond paste and return to a boil, mashing some of the berries against the side of the pan. Cover, reduce the heat and simmer for 15 minutes. Add the wine and simmer for 5 minutes more.

Remove the cinnamon stick and serve.

BORSCHT WITH HAZELNUT CREAM

4 medium-size beets (about 2 pounds)

1 tablespoon unsalted butter

1 small onion, chopped

$^1/_2$ cup chopped carrot

1 small garlic clove, chopped

1 teaspoon granulated sugar

$^1/_3$ teaspoon ground cloves

3 cups chicken broth

1 tablespoon fresh lemon juice

salt and freshly ground white pepper to taste

$^3/_4$ cup shelled, roasted and peeled hazelnuts

$^3/_4$ cup sour cream

snipped fresh chives for garnish

Serves 6

Preparation time: 1 hour 15 minutes, plus several hours or overnight to chill

Trim the beets, leaving the roots and 2 inches of the stems attached. Scrub them well, put them in a large pot and cover them with cold water. Bring the water to a boil, cover, lower the heat and simmer for 25 to 30 minutes, until the beets are tender. Drop the beets into cold water and let sit until they are cool enough to handle. Peel and cut them into $^1/_2$-inch dice. Set aside.

In a 3-quart saucepan, melt the butter over medium heat. Sauté the onion and carrot for about 7 minutes, until the onion is soft and translucent. Add the garlic, sugar, cloves, reserved beets, and broth. Bring to a boil, cover, lower the heat and simmer for about 20 minutes. Purée half the cooked mixture in a blender or food processor fitted with a steel blade. Pour it into a bowl or container and then process the remaining soup. Add lemon juice and salt and pepper to taste.

Cover and cool the puréed soup. Refrigerate it for several hours or overnight.

Shortly before serving, place the hazelnuts in a blender or food processor fitted with a steel blade and process until they are puréed, stopping occasionally to scrape the sides. Add the sour cream and process until just combined. Refrigerate until serving time.

Serve the soup cold in bowls topped with a dollop of hazelnut cream and some snipped chives.

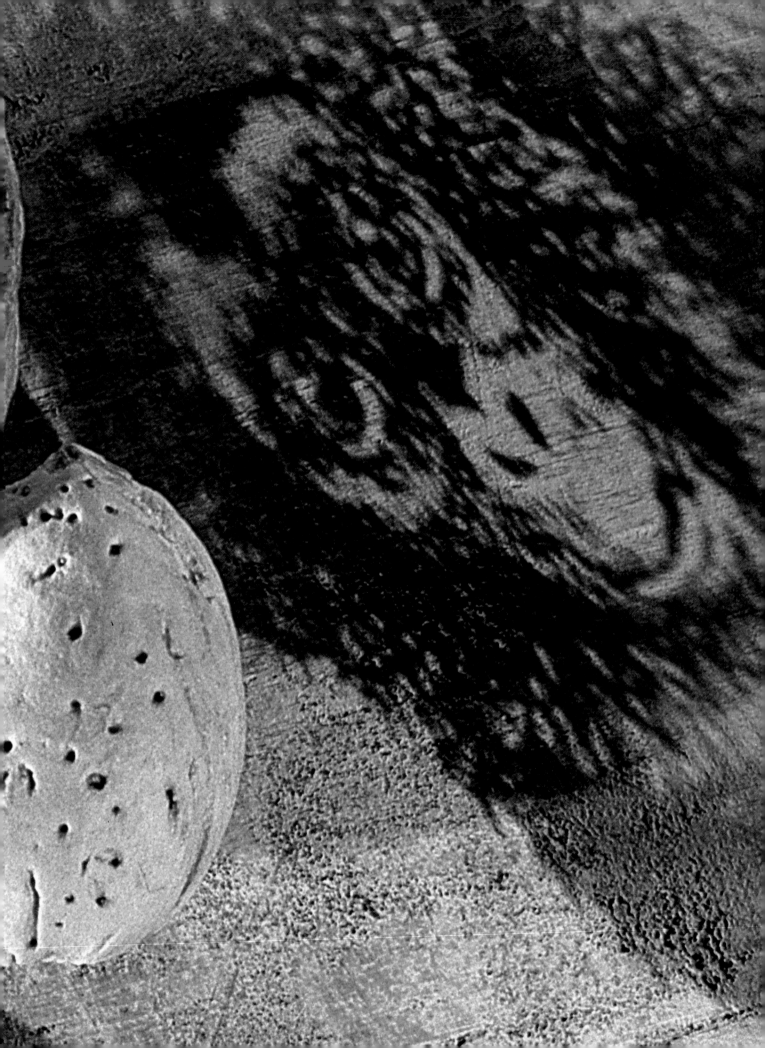

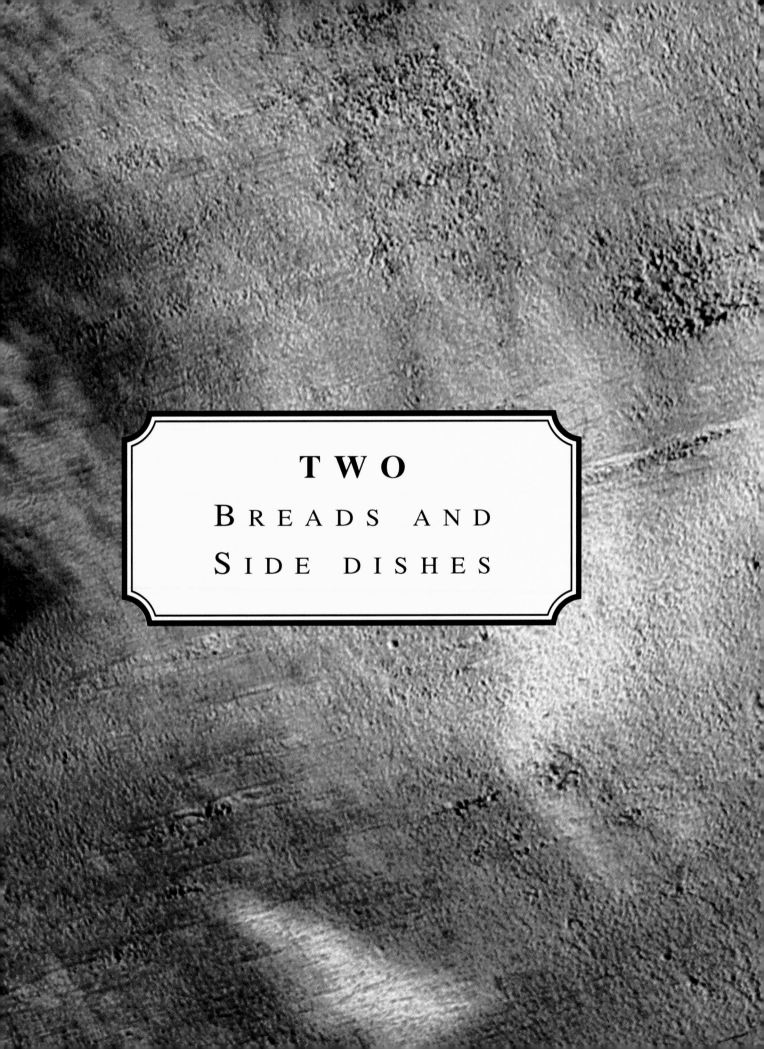

TWO
BREADS AND
SIDE DISHES

PEANUT BUTTER BISCUITS

1¹/4 cups unbleached all-purpose flour

1 tablespoon baking powder

¹/2 teaspoon baking soda

¹/2 teaspoon salt

³/4 cup whole wheat flour

³/4 cup crunchy peanut butter (made without sugar or salt)

³/4 cup buttermilk

1 tablespoon honey

Makes 8 or 9 biscuits

Preparation time: 30 minutes

Preheat the oven to 450º. Grease a 9-inch round cake pan.

Sift together the all-purpose flour, baking powder, baking soda and salt. Add the whole wheat flour and stir to blend. With a pastry blender, your fingers, or 2 knives, cut the peanut butter into the dry ingredients until they are thoroughly dispersed.

Combine the buttermilk and honey, add the mixture to the dough, and stir until combined.

Turn the dough onto a floured board or counter and knead for 30 seconds. Roll or pat out to a 1-inch thickness. Cut the dough with a 2¹/2-inch biscuit cutter or an inverted floured drinking glass.

Place the biscuits, evenly spaced, in the prepared pan and bake for 12 to 15 minutes, until golden brown. Serve hot.

DATE AND PISTACHIO SCONES

2¹/2 cups unbleached all-purpose flour

¹/3 cup firmly packed dark brown sugar

2¹/2 teaspoons baking powder

¹/2 teaspoon baking soda

¹/2 teaspoon salt

¹/4 teaspoon ground cinnamon

grated zest of 1 lemon

¹/2 cup unsalted butter, frozen (cold if you are not using a food processor)

³/4 cup buttermilk

1¹/2 teaspoons vanilla extract

1¹/2 pound pitted dates, chopped

1 cup shelled and peeled pistachios

1 large egg yolk

¹/2 teaspoon water

Makes 15 scones

Preparation time: 45 minutes

Preheat the oven to 400º. Grease a cookie sheet or large pizza pan.

In a food processor fitted with a steel blade (or in a large bowl if you are making the dough by hand), place the flour, brown sugar, baking powder, baking soda, salt, cinnamon and lemon zest. Pulse for 1 to 2 seconds or stir together. If processing, cut the frozen butter into 8 pieces and add it to the bowl. Process, pulsing on and off, just until the mixture resembles coarse meal. Do not over-process. (By hand, cut the cold butter into ¹/2-inch dice and work into the flour mixture with a pastry blender, 2 knives or your fingers until it resembles coarse meal.)

Combine the buttermilk and vanilla extract. With the motor running, add the liquid all at once to the food processor and process just until the mixture forms a ball. (By hand, stir in the liquids and mix until thoroughly combined.) Turn the dough out onto a floured board. Mix in the dates and all but 3 tablespoons of the nuts by hand until well distributed. On a floured board, pat or roll out the dough to a ³/4-inch thickness. Cut it into 3-inch triangles with a sharp knife. Place 1 inch apart in the prepared pan.

Beat the egg yolk with the water and brush it over the top of each scone. Chop the reserved nuts and sprinkle over the top.

Bake for 15 to 20 minutes, until lightly browned and a toothpick inserted in the middle comes out clean. Cool for 5 minutes. Serve immediately cutting the scones apart if necessary or separate and cool completely on a wire rack. Store in an airtight container.

Blueberry and Almond Muffins

1¼ cups unbleached all-purpose flour

2 teaspoons baking powder

½ teaspoon ground cinnamon

½ teaspoon salt

2 cup granulated sugar

1 large egg

4 tablespoons unsalted butter, melted

⅓ cup milk

1 teaspoon grated lemon zest

½ teaspoon almond extract

1 cup fresh or unthawed blueberries

1 cup shelled, toasted and coarsely chopped almonds

Makes 6 muffins

Preparation time: 40 minutes

Preheat the oven to 400º. Grease and flour 6 3-inch muffin cups.

Sift the flour, baking powder, cinnamon and salt together into a large mixing bowl.

In another bowl, whisk together the sugar and egg until the mixture is pale and lemon-colored. Whisk in the melted butter and milk and then the lemon zest and almond extract.

Gently stir the liquid mixture into the dry mixture, stirring just until the dry ingredients are thoroughly moistened but still lumpy. Fold in the berries and nuts just until they are evenly distributed. Do not overmix.

Fill the muffin cups to the top and bake for 20 to 25 minutes or until the muffins are golden brown and spring back when pressed lightly. Cool, at least slightly, in the pan or on wire racks. Serve while still warm or at room temperature. The muffins may be stored in an airtight container and reheated if desired.

Hazelnut and Honey Muffins

1½ cups unbleached all-purpose flour

1 tablespoon baking powder

1½ cups rolled oats

½ teaspoon baking soda

½ teaspoon salt

1 cup plain yogurt

½ cup honey

1½ teaspoons vanilla extract

1 large egg

¼ cup hazelnut oil (vegetable oil may be substituted)

1½ cups coarsely chopped roasted hazelnuts

Makes 1 dozen muffins

Preparation time: 45 minutes

Preheat the oven to 450º. Grease a dozen 2½-inch muffin cups.

In a large mixing bowl, combine the flour, baking powder, oats, baking soda and salt. Mix well.

In another bowl, whisk together the yogurt, honey, vanilla extract, egg and oil.

Combine the dry and wet ingredients, stirring just until the dry ingredients are thoroughly moistened. Fold in the toasted hazelnuts just until they are well distributed. Do not overmix. The batter should be lumpy.

Heap the mixture into the muffin cups so it is about ½-inch above the top of the pan and evenly distributed. Bake for 18 to 20 minutes or until the muffins are golden brown and spring back when pressed lightly.

Remove from the pan and cool on a wire rack for at least 5 minutes. Serve warm or cool. Store in an airtight container. The muffins may be reheated if desired.

PECAN AND PROSCIUTTO BREAD

6 ounces prosciutto, chopped

5 tablespoons unsalted butter, margarine

or vegetable shortening at room temperature

1¼ cups warm water

1 ¼-ounce envelope active dry yeast

2 teaspoons granulated sugar

4½ cups bread flour (unbleached all-purpose flour may be substituted, with some loss in rising)

1½ teaspoons freshly cracked black pepper

1½ cups coarsely chopped pecans

2 teaspoons cornmeal

Makes 1 baguette
Preparation time: 3 hours

Grease the inside of a large bowl. Set aside.

Sauté the prosciutto in a skillet in ½ tablespoon of the butter over medium heat for about 2 minutes. Pour the meat and butter into a large ungreased mixing bowl. Add the warm water yeast and sugar to the bowl. Stir to combine. Mix in 1 cup of the flour and 4 tablespoons of the remaining butter. Stir until well combined. Add the pepper, pecans and 3 cups of the remaining flour. Mix well. Spread ⅓ cup flour on your work surface and turn the dough out onto it. Knead, incorporating more flour as needed to keep the dough from sticking. Do not use any more flour than necessary. Knead for about 5 minutes, until the dough is smooth and elastic.

Form the dough into a ball and place it in the greased bowl. Turn the dough over so it is greased on all sides, cover the bowl and let the dough rise in a warm place until doubled in size, about 1 hour to 1 hour 30 minutes.

Sprinkle the cornmeal over a baking sheet or baguette pan. Set aside.

Melt the remaining ½ tablespoon of butter and set aside.

When the dough has doubled, punch it down with your fist and turn it out onto a lightly floured surface. Roll or pat the dough into a 10- x 15-inch rectangle. Roll the dough up tightly, jelly-roll fashion. Pinch the ends and the edges of the dough to seal it. Place it on the prepared pan, seam down, with the ends tucked under it. Brush it with the melted butter. Cover it loosely with plastic wrap and let it rise in a warm place until it has again doubled in size, about 30 minutes. About halfway through the second rise, preheat the oven to 375º.

Bake the bread for about 30 minutes, until it is browned and sounds hollow when tapped. Cool on a wire rack.

CURRIED CORN AND COCONUT TIMBALES

$1^1/_2$ cups fresh corn kernels, cut or grated from the cob (about 6 ears)

3 large eggs

$^1/_3$ cup fresh crustless white bread crumbs

2 tablespoons grated onion

$^1/_2$ cup freshly grated coconut

$^1/_2$ cup coconut milk

$^1/_3$ teaspoon salt

1 teaspoon good-quality curry powder

$^1/_4$ teaspoon freshly ground white pepper

$^1/_2$ cup shredded and toasted unsweetened coconut for garnish (optional)

Serves 6

Preparation time: 50 minutes

Preheat the oven to 350º. Butter 6 6-ounce custard cups and set aside.

In a mixing bowl, combine all the ingredients except the toasted coconut. Mix thoroughly. Pour the mixture into the prepared custard cups, filling them about $^3/_4$ full.

Place the custard cups in a roasting pan and pour enough water into the pan to reach halfway up the sides of the cups. Bake the timbales for 5 minutes, then lower the oven temperature to 325º and continue to bake for 25 to 30 minutes, until the timbales are set and a toothpick inserted in the center comes out clean.

Cool the timbales in the cups for 10 minutes. Then serve, either in the cups or inverted and unmolded onto plates. Top with toasted coconut if desired.

BRAISED CHESTNUTS WITH ONIONS AND PRUNES

$^1/_4$ cup bacon grease or unsalted butter

1 pound chestnuts, shelled and peeled

1 pound small white onions, peeled

2 cups beef broth

1 cup good-quality port wine

$^1/_4$ cup firmly packed dark brown sugar

1 bay leaf

$^1/_2$ pound pitted prunes

salt and freshly ground black pepper to taste

In a large, heavy sauté pan, melt 2 tablespoons of the grease or butter over medium heat and sauté the chestnuts until lightly browned, about 7 minutes. Remove with a slotted spoon and reserve.

Add another tablespoon of the grease or butter and sauté the onions until lightly browned, about 5 to 7 minutes. Return the chestnuts to the pan and add the broth, port, brown sugar and bay leaf. Bring to a boil, then lower the heat and simmer for 30 minutes, stirring gently several times. Add the prunes and return to a simmer. Continue to simmer stirring gently several times, for 30 to 35 minutes more or until the liquid has formed a syrupy glaze.

Remove the bay leaf, season to taste with salt and pepper and serve hot. This recipe may be made a day in advance and reheated by adding $^1/_2$ cup more broth and cooking on low heat until the syrupy glaze has re-formed.

Serves 6

Preparation time: 1 hour 20 minutes

VIDALIA ONIONS STUFFED WITH APPLES AND CASHEWS

6 well-formed large fresh Vidalia or other sweet onions (about 3 inches in diameter)

salt and freshly ground black pepper to taste

6 tablespoons unsalted butter at room temperature

2 medium-size tart apples, such as Granny Smith

$^2/_3$ cup chopped roasted cashews

3 tablespoons finely chopped parsley

$1^1/_2$ teaspoons finely chopped fresh tarragon (or $^1/_2$ teaspoon dried)

1-$1^1/_2$ cups dry white wine

Serves 6

Preparation time: 1 hour 45 minutes

Preheat the oven to 350º.

Trim the root end of each onion slightly to make a flat base. Slice off the other end leaving a cut surface 2 to $2^1/_2$ inches in diameter. Peel each onion and dig out the flesh with a melon baller leaving the bottoms and sides about $^3/_8$ inch thick. Chop $1^1/_2$ cups of the onion flesh, and salt and pepper the inside of the onions. In a skillet, melt 4 tablespoons of the butter over medium heat. Sauté the chopped onion for about 5 minutes, stirring frequently. Peel, core and chop the apples and add them to the pan. Sauté for about 10 minutes more, until just beginning to brown. Remove from the heat.

Stir in all but 2 tablespoons of the cashews to the onion and apple mixture, then the parsley and tarragon.

Melt 1 tablespoon of the remaining butter. Reserve.

With the remaining tablespoon of butter, butter the outsides of the cored onions and the inside of a pan just large enough to hold them. Pack the onions with the stuffing (don't press too hard), and place them in the prepared pan. Top with the reserved cashews and drizzle with the melted butter.

Bring the wine to a boil in a small saucepan and pour it $^1/_2$ to 1 inch deep around the onions. Place the pan in the lower part of your oven. Bake for about 1 hour basting frequently, or until the onions are tender.

TOMATOES STUFFED WITH SAFFRON RICE AND BRAZIL NUTS

6 large ripe but firm tomatoes (approximately 3 inches in diameter)

1 teaspoon salt

$1^1/_2$ cups chicken broth

$^1/_2$ teaspoon saffron threads, crushed

2 tablespoons olive oil

$^3/_4$ cup chopped Brazil nuts, plus 6 whole shelled nuts

$^1/_4$ cup chopped shallot

$^3/_4$ cup long-grain rice

3 tablespoons chopped fresh parsley

freshly ground black pepper to taste

Serves 6

Preparation time: 1 hour 15 minutes

Preheat the oven to 350º.

Lightly oil a baking dish just large enough to hold the tomatoes. Cut the stem end from each tomato. Carefully scrape out the seeds and pulp.

Salt the insides of the tomatoes and invert them on paper towels to drain.

In a small saucepan, bring the chicken broth to a boil, remove from the heat, and add the saffron and set aside.

Heat the olive oil in a 1-quart saucepan over medium-high heat and sauté the chopped Brazil nuts, stirring often, until lightly browned, about 1 to 2 minutes. Remove with a slotted spoon to paper towels to drain.

Sauté the shallot in the same oil over medium heat for 1 minute. Add the rice and sauté for a moment, stirring constantly. Add the broth and bring to a boil. Then cover the pan and simmer for 15 to 20 minutes, until all the liquid is absorbed.

Mix the chopped nuts, parsley and pepper into the cooked rice. Stuff each tomato with the rice mixture and top each with one of the whole Brazil nuts. Place the tomatoes in the prepared baking dish. Bake for 25 minutes. Serve warm or at room temperature.

ORZO WITH PANCETTA AND PINE NUTS

$^1/_4$ pound pancetta (other unsmoked bacon may be substituted)

2 tablespoons olive oil

$^1/_2$ cup pine nuts

1 cup orzo

2 cups chicken broth

$1^1/_2$ teaspoons chopped fresh oregano leaves (or $^1/_2$ teaspoon dried)

salt and freshly ground black pepper to taste

Serves 4

Preparation time: 30 minutes

Chop the pancetta and sauté it in the olive oil in a medium-size saucepan over medium heat until lightly browned. Remove with a slotted spoon to paper towels to drain. Add the pine nuts to the pan and sauté, stirring constantly until browned, about 1 to 2 minutes. Remove with a slotted spoon to paper towels to drain. Add the orzo to the pan and sauté for about 1 minute, stirring constantly.

Add the broth, oregano, salt and pepper then bring the mixture to a boil. Lower the heat, cover the pan and simmer for 12 to 14 minutes, until all the broth is absorbed. Remove the pan from the heat.

Return the pancetta and pine nuts to the pan. Toss and serve.

BARLEY WITH WILD MUSHROOMS AND CHESTNUTS

$^1/_2$ pound chestnuts, shelled and peeled

1 tablespoon olive oil

$^1/_4$ pound fresh wild mushrooms, such as chanterelles, shiitake, morels or oyster, stems removed, sliced

3 tablespoons unsalted butter

2 large shallots, minced

$^1/_3$ cup chopped carrot

$^1/_3$ cup chopped celery

$^1/_4$ cup dry vermouth

1 cup pearl barley

$1^1/_2$ teaspoons chopped fresh thyme leaves (or $^1/_2$ teaspoon dried)

$3^1/_2$ cups rich chicken broth, boiling

Serves 8

Preparation time: 1 hour

Preheat the oven to 350º.

Slice the chestnuts and set aside. Heat the oil in a flameproof 2- or 3-quart casserole with a lid over medium-high heat. Sauté the mushrooms until lightly browned (about 4 to 5 minutes). Remove and reserve.

Lower the heat to medium, add the butter, shallots, carrot and celery and sauté until the shallots are translucent, about 3 to 5 minutes. Add the vermouth, raise the heat and bring the liquid to a boil. Add the barley thyme, boiling broth and reserved mushrooms and chestnuts. Cover and bake for 45 minutes. Remove from the oven, stir, replace the cover and let sit for 5 minutes before serving.

YAMS WITH BOURBON AND PECANS

4 tablespoons unsalted butter

1^{1}/$_{2}$ pounds yams, peeled and cut into
^{1}/$_{2}$-inch dice (about 5 cups)

^{1}/$_{2}$ cup bourbon

1 tablespoon granulated sugar

2 tablespoons fresh lemon juice salt and
freshly ground black pepper to taste

^{3}/$_{4}$ cup coarsely chopped roasted pecans

Serves 4 to 6

Preparation time: 20 minutes

In a large skillet, melt the butter over medium-high heat and sauté the yams, stirring constantly for about 5 minutes. Stir in the remaining ingredients, cover the skillet, lower the heat and simmer for 5 minutes more. Remove the lid, raise the heat to medium and cook until the liquid is almost all gone, stirring often. Serve at once.

THREE

MAIN

COURSES

LAMB IN MACADAMIA CREAM SAUCE

1¼ cups macadamia nuts

2 medium-size onions, each cut into 16 pieces

1½ tablespoons chopped fresh ginger

1 cup plain yogurt

2 tablespoons ground coriander

1 tablespoon ground cardamom

1 teaspoon freshly ground black pepper

1 cup heavy cream

½ cup raisins

2½ pounds boneless leg of lamb, trimmed of all fat and cut into 1½-inch cubes

salt to taste

chopped cilantro or parsley leaves for garnish

With a sharp knife, thinly slice ¼ cup of the macadamia nuts. Don't worry if pieces crumble; ideally however they should resemble shaved chocolate. Refrigerate in an airtight container until needed.

Place the remaining cup of nuts in a blender or food processor fitted with a steel blade along with the onions, ginger and yogurt. Process, stopping to scrape the bowl occasionally until the mixture resembles cooked oatmeal.

Place the purée in a large, heavy saucepan or skillet along with the coriander, cardamom, pepper, heavy cream, raisins and lamb. Bring to a simmer over medium heat. Lower the heat, cover and simmer for 1 hour 30 minutes, stirring gently often during cooking to prevent sticking.

Uncover, add salt to taste and raise the heat slightly. Continue to simmer for 30 to 45 minutes more, until the meat is very tender and the sauce has thickened. This dish is best made early in the day and allowed to mellow at room temperature, then reheated gently. Or it may be made a day in advance and refrigerated before reheating.

Serve with rice if desired, garnished with the reserved sliced macadamias and the chopped cilantro or parsley.

Serves 6 to 8

Preparation time: 2 hours 30 minutes

HAZELNUT STROGANOFF

4 tablespoons unsalted butter

1½ pounds beef filet or boned porterhouse, trimmed of all fat and cut into 2- x ½-inch strips

1 medium-size onion, halved and thinly sliced

1 tablespoon unbleached all-purpose flour

1 teaspoon Dijon mustard

1 cup beef broth

½ cup sour cream

1 cup shelled, roasted and peeled hazelnuts

coarsely ground salt and freshly ground black pepper to taste

Serves 6

Preparation time: 30 minutes

In a heavy skillet, heat 1 tablespoon of the butter over high heat and add half the meat, stirring constantly until lightly browned, about 1 to 2 minutes. Pour the meat and butter into a bowl.

Place another tablespoon of the butter in the skillet and repeat the procedure with the rest of the meat. When all the meat is in the bowl, add the remaining 2 tablespoons butter to the skillet and lower the heat to medium. Sauté the onion, stirring frequently until tender, about 5 minutes.

Add the flour to the onion and mix well. Add the mustard and then the broth and stir constantly until the mixture thickens slightly about 5 to 7 minutes. Stir in the sour cream, half the hazelnuts, the reserved meat and the salt and pepper. Heat over low heat, stirring often, until heated through. Do not boil.

Serve as is or over rice or egg noodles, garnished with the remaining hazelnuts.

TAGLIATELLE WITH CHESTNUTS AND SAUSAGE

³/₄ pound fresh chestnuts, roasted, shelled and peeled

3 cups chicken broth

1 small bay leaf

1 whole clove

1 small shallot, peeled

¹/₂ teaspoon ground cardamom

1 cup heavy cream

¹/₂ pound hot Italian sausage

1 pound tagliatelle

2 tablespoons unsalted butter, melted

2 tablespoons chopped fresh parsley

freshly ground black pepper to taste

Serves 4 to 6

Preparation time: 1 hour

Place the chestnuts, broth, bay leaf, clove and shallot in a small saucepan. Bring the broth to a boil, cover and reduce the heat. Simmer for 35 to 40 minutes, until the chestnuts are very tender.

Remove the bay leaf and clove. Place the chestnuts and shallot with about half the broth in the bowl of a blender or food processor fitted with a steel blade. Process, scraping down the sides of the bowl several times, until the mixture is thick and smooth. Add the remaining broth, cardamom and cream and process until smooth and well combined. (The sauce can be made in advance to this point and refrigerated.)

Place the mixture in a saucepan and heat over low heat until steaming.

Heat a medium-size skillet over medium high heat. Cut the casings off the sausage and crumble it into the pan. Sauté, continuing to break the sausage apart with a spoon, until browned. Remove with a slotted spoon to paper towels to drain. Reserve.

Prepare the tagliatelle according to the package directions, cooking until *al dente*. Drain. Toss it with the melted butter.

Arrange the pasta on plates or a serving platter and top with the sauce. Then scatter the sausage and parsley on top. Add pepper to taste.

GRILLED SALMON ON COCONUT CABBAGE

6 salmon steaks (about 6 ounces each)

3 cups coconut milk

2 tablespoons fresh lime juice

3 tablespoons olive oil

1 large onion, halved and thinly sliced

1 teaspoon crushed red pepper flakes

$1/2$ teaspoon ground ginger

1 small head of green cabbage (about $2^1/2$ pounds)

salt and freshly ground black pepper to taste

1 cup shredded fresh coconut

Serves 6

Preparation time: 1 hour 10 minutes

Place the salmon steaks in a dish or pan just large enough to hold them. Combine 1 cup of the coconut milk with 1 tablespoon of the lime juice and pour the mixture over the steaks. Marinate in refrigerator for 1 hour.

In a 12-inch sauté pan or skillet, heat the olive oil over medium heat. Add the onion, crushed red pepper and ginger and sauté, stirring frequently until the onion begins to brown, about 8 to 10 minutes.

Pull the outer leaves from the head of cabbage and discard. Quarter the cabbage, then trim away and discard most of the core. Thinly slice the cabbage quarters crosswise. You should have about 8 or 9 cups of cabbage. Add the cabbage to the sauté pan in batches, about a cup at a time, cooking down as necessary and stirring well. Cover and lower the heat to medium-low. Cook for 5 minutes, then uncover the pan. The volume should have been reduced significantly. Continue to cook, uncovered, stirring often, until the cabbage is lightly browned and limp, about 15 to 20 minutes.

Add the remaining coconut milk and lime juice along with the salt and black pepper to taste. Reserve $1/4$ cup of the shredded coconut for garnish and add the rest to the pan, stirring well. Simmer, uncovered, stirring occasionally until the liquid is reduced to a creamy sauce, about 10 minutes. (The cabbage may be made to this point in advance and reheated slowly as the fish grills.)

Remove the salmon steaks from the marinade, reserving the marinade. Season the steaks with salt and pepper to taste. Grill over hot coals or under a broiler, basting a couple of times with the reserved marinade, until the salmon turns a much paler color, about 3 to 5 minutes on each side.

Arrange the cabbage on serving plates or a large platter. Top with the salmon steaks. Garnish with sprinkles of the reserved coconut.

SCALLOPS WITH LEMON AND PISTACHIOS

4 tablespoons unsalted butter

1¹/₂ tablespoons finely chopped shallot

1¹/₂ pounds scallops (bay scallops left whole, sea scallops halved)

4 cup fresh lemon juice

¹/₂ cup shelled, peeled and roasted pistachios

salt and freshly ground black pepper to taste

lemon slices for garnish (optional)

Serves 4 to 6

Preparation time: 10 minutes

Melt the butter in a large skillet over medium heat. Add the shallot and scallops and sauté until the scallops are opaque, about 3 to 5 minutes. Add the lemon juice and pistachios. Toss to combine. Heat through and season to taste with salt and pepper.

Serve garnished with lemon slices if desired.

SPINACH FETTUCCINE WITH STILTON AND PECANS

2 teaspoons salt

1 pound spinach fettuccine

1/3 cup olive oil

1 garlic clove, crushed

2 tablespoons balsamic vinegar

1/2 pound Stilton cheese

salt and freshly ground black pepper to taste

1 cup roasted pecan halves, broken into large pieces

Bring a large pot of water to a boil. Add the salt and the fettuccine and boil until *al dente* (approximately 1 to 3 minutes if fresh; according to package directions if dried).

At the same time, in a small saucepan or skillet, heat the olive oil over medium high heat. Add the garlic and sauté until the edges are brown, about 2 to 4 minutes. Remove the garlic and discard. Remove the oil from the heat. When the fettuccine is *al dente*, drain it and return it to the pot or place it in a bowl. Add the hot oil along with the vinegar. Toss to coat. Crumble the cheese over the mixture, add salt and pepper to taste and toss again to mix and to melt the cheese.

Divide the pasta among serving plates. Top with the pecans and serve.

Serves 4 to 6

Preparation time: 25 minutes

TURKEY WITH WALNUT MOLE SAUCE

2 large poblano or Anaheim chilies

3 tablespoons olive oil

1 large garlic clove, minced

1 cup chopped onion

$^1/_2$ cup chopped celery

1/3 cup chopped carrot

$^1/_2$ teaspoon cayenne pepper

$^1/_2$ teaspoon ground cardamom

pinch of ground cloves

$^1/_2$ cup good-quality port wine

1 ounce unsweetened chocolate, chopped

1$^1/_4$ cups chicken broth

salt and freshly ground black pepper to taste

1 5-pound turkey breast

$^3/_4$ cup chopped walnuts

$^1/_4$ cup chopped cilantro

Serves 8 to 10

Preparation time: 50 minutes, plus the time to cook the turkey

Wash and dry the chilies. Over the flame of a gas burner or under a broiler, char the skins of the peppers, turning them with tongs as they blacken. Wet 2 paper towels, squeeze them dry and unwad them. Lay one on the counter. Place the charred peppers on the towel, cover them with the second towel and let them cool for a few minutes.

Uncover the peppers and scrape off the charred skins with the edge of a knife. Slice the peppers in half lengthwise. Remove and discard the cores and seeds. Chop and reserve the peppers. Heat the oil in a sauté pan over medium heat. Add the garlic and onion and sauté until the edges of the onion begin to turn golden, about 10 minutes. Add the celery and carrot and sauté, stirring often, for 2 more minutes. Add the cayenne, cardamom, cloves and reserved peppers and stir to combine. Add the port and raise the heat, stirring until all the liquid has evaporated. Add the chocolate, stirring to combine. Then add the broth and bring to a boil, stirring often. Lower the heat and simmer, uncovered, for 20 minutes or until the vegetables are tender.

Purée this sauce in a blender or food processor fitted with a steel blade. Return it to the sauté pan or refrigerate it until serving time and reheat gently stirring often. Season to taste with salt and pepper.

Roast, boil or sauté the turkey breast, whole or sliced, according to your preference. Serve each portion of turkey topped with the mole sauce and sprinkled with the walnuts and chopped cilantro.

Catfish Amandine

4 catfish fillets (about 6 ounces each)

¹/₂ cup milk

¹/₃ cup unbleached all-purpose flour

¹/₄ teaspoon salt

¹/₄ teaspoon freshly ground black pepper

4 tablespoons unsalted butter

¹/₂ cup sliced almonds

1 tablespoon olive oil

¹/₄ cup dry vermouth or dry white wine

Serves 4

Preparation time: 1 hour 15 minutes

Soak the catfish fillets in the milk for 1 hour in the refrigerator. Drain and pat dry.

Combine the flour, salt and pepper. Dredge the fillets in the mixture and place them on a piece of wax paper or plastic wrap. In a large, heavy skillet, heat 1 tablespoon of the butter over medium heat. Add the almonds and sauté until golden brown, about 1 to 2 minutes, stirring frequently. Remove with a slotted spoon to paper towels to drain. Add 2 more tablespoons of butter and the olive oil to the skillet and raise the heat to medium-high. Sauté the fish fillets until golden brown, about 2 to 3 minutes, then turn them over and sauté the other side for 2 to 3 minutes, until golden brown. Remove to a heated serving plate.

Wipe out the pan and add the last tablespoon of butter and the vermouth or wine, stirring until thoroughly combined. Pour the sauce over the fillets. Sprinkle the almonds over the top. Serve hot.

PEANUT CHILI

1 pound roasted shelled peanuts

3 tablespoons peanut oil

2 cups chopped onion

4 garlic cloves, chopped

1 1/2 cups chopped green bell pepper

1 1/2 cups chopped celery

1 cup chopped carrot

2 jalapeno or serrano chilies, seeded and chopped

2 tablespoons chili powder

1/2 teaspoon cayenne pepper (or more to taste)

1 tablespoon ground cumin

2 tablespoons chopped fresh oregano

(or 1 tablespoon dried)

2 tablespoons chopped fresh basil

(or 1 tablespoon dried)

3 1/2 cups fresh or canned peeled, seeded and chopped tomatoes with liquid

3 1/2 cups chicken or vegetable broth

2 tablespoons molasses

salt and freshly ground black pepper to taste

shredded Monterey Jack cheese or queso blanco

finely chopped cilantro

Serves 6 to 8

Preparation time: 1 hour

Place 1/2 cup of the peanuts in a blender or food processor fitted with a steel blade and process very briefly pulsing on and off until the nuts are coarsely chopped. Set aside. Place the remaining nuts in the blender or food processor and process, pulsing on and off, until the nuts are very finely chopped and cling together in clumps. Set aside.

In a heavy 4-quart soup pot, heat the oil over medium-high heat. Add the onion and garlic and sauté for several minutes, stirring often, until the onion begins to look translucent. Add the bell pepper, celery, carrot, and jalapeno or serrano chilies and sauté for 5 to 7 minutes more, stirring frequently. Add the chili powder, cayenne, cumin, oregano and basil, stirring thoroughly to combine. Add the tomatoes, finely chopped peanuts, broth, and molasses. Bring to a boil, cover, lower the heat and simmer for 30 minutes. Salt and pepper to taste. Like all chili, this is best made in advance and reheated slowly stirring frequently. Serve hot, garnished with shredded cheese, chopped cilantro, and reserved coarsely chopped peanuts. Serve with rice if desired.

OPAL BASIL AND SUN-DRIED TOMATO PESTO WITH WALNUTS AND PINE NUTS

1 cup fresh purple basil leaves, washed and dried

2 garlic cloves, crushed

$^1/_4$ cup sun-dried tomatoes packed in olive oil, drained, patted dry and chopped

$^1/_2$ cup shelled walnuts

$^1/_3$ cup toasted pine nuts

$^1/_2$ cup extra-virgin olive oil

$^1/_2$ cup grated Parmesan cheese

salt and freshly ground black pepper to taste

Makes $1^1/_4$ cups

Preparation time: 10 minutes

This recipe makes enough pesto sauce for 1 pound of pasta. For variations, you may use it on chicken, in omelets, or on bruschetta.

In the bowl of a blender or food processor fitted with a steel blade, combine the basil leaves, garlic, sun-dried tomatoes, walnuts and pine nuts. Process to chop the ingredients, stopping to scrape down the sides of the bowl. Turn the motor back on and add the olive oil in a thin stream. Once the oil is incorporated, stop the motor and add the cheese and salt and pepper to taste. Process again, just until combined.

Use the pesto immediately or refrigerate in an airtight container.

STIR-FRIED VEAL WITH CASHEWS

1¹/₂ pounds boneless veal loin, bottom round, sirloin or shoulder, trimmed of fat and cut into ³/₄-inch cubes

1 tablespoon cornstarch

1 large egg white

¹/₄ cup peanut oil

1 cup raw cashews

1 1-inch piece fresh ginger, finely chopped

3 scallions, sliced, white and green portions kept separate

¹/₂ red bell pepper, cut into thin strips 1¹/₂ inches long

¹/₄ pound snow peas, stems and strings removed, halved diagonally

1 tablespoon dry sherry

1 teaspoon granulated sugar

¹/₂ teaspoon salt

1 teaspoon dark sesame oil (available at Asian and specialty markets)

Serves 4 to 6
Preparation time: 35 minutes

Place the veal cubes in a small bowl. Add the cornstarch and toss to coat. Add the egg white and toss again. Let sit for 15 to 20 minutes.

Heat the peanut oil in a wok or large skillet over medium heat. When hot, add the cashews and fry them, stirring until they are lightly browned, about 2 to 3 minutes. Remove the nuts with a slotted spoon to a paper towel to drain.

Raise the heat to medium-high and add the veal cubes, stir-frying until cooked through. Remove with a slotted spoon to a small bowl and reserve.

Add the ginger and the white parts of the scallions to the oil and stir-fry for 1 minute. Add the bell pepper and snow peas and stir-fry for 1 minute more. Add the veal, sherry sugar and salt and toss to coat thoroughly, about 1 minute. Add the cashews, sesame oil and green parts of the scallions, toss and serve.

Serve as is or over rice.

FOUR
Salads

THAI-STYLE PEANUT SALAD

Salad:

1 head romaine lettuce, washed and dried

$^1/_2$ cup fresh mint leaves, washed, dried and coarsely chopped

$^1/_2$ cup cilantro leaves, washed, dried and coarsely chopped

1 7-inch-long cucumber, peeled, halved lengthwise, seeded and thinly sliced

2 medium-size tomatoes, cut into thin wedges

2 cups mung bean sprouts, rinsed and drained

1 medium-size red onion, thinly sliced

1 cup roasted shelled peanuts, coarsely chopped

Dressing:

5 tablespoons fresh lime juice

3 tablespoons fish sauce (available at specialty stores and Asian markets)

$1^1/_2$ teaspoons granulated sugar

1 teaspoon soy sauce

1 teaspoon red chili paste (available at specialty stores and Asian markets)

1 garlic clove, minced

$^1/_3$ cup peanut oil

salt and freshly ground black pepper to taste

Serves 4 to 6

Preparation time: 15 minutes

Tear the lettuce into pieces and arrange on a large platter or individual plates. Scatter the mint and cilantro leaves over them. Scatter the cucumber slices over the leaves and arrange the tomato wedges around the edges. Pile the bean sprouts in the center. Arrange the onion rings over the top. Sprinkle with the peanuts.

Combine the dressing ingredients in a jar and shake well. Drizzle over the salad and serve.

FENNEL, ORANGE AND ALMOND SALAD

2 medium-size fennel bulbs with feathery tops
2 oranges
2 scallions, thinly sliced
2 tablespoons fresh lemon juice
1/4 cup almond or olive oil
1 tablespoon honey
salt and freshly ground black pepper to taste
2/3 cup sliced toasted almonds

Serves 6 to 8
Preparation time: 15 minutes

Trim the bulbs of any blemishes and cut off the stalks above the bulbs, reserving any feathery green leaves. Cut each bulb lengthwise into quarters and cut out the hard core. Slice each quarter crosswise into 1/4-inch-thick slices. Place them in a serving bowl.

Grate enough zest from the oranges to make 1 teaspoon. Reserve.

Chop 3 tablespoons of the fennel tops. Reserve.

Peel the oranges with a sharp paring knife, cutting through the peel and pith, just to the flesh at one end, and spiralling down and around as if peeling an apple. Insert the knife along the membranes between sections, separating and popping out the sections. Remove and discard any seeds and add the sections to the fennel. Sprinkle with the scallions and chill until serving time.

When ready to serve, combine the lemon juice, oil, reserved zest, honey, salt and pepper in a small jar, cruet or bowl. Shake or whisk to blend. Toss the salad with the dressing and serve garnished with the nuts and reserved chopped fennel tops.

ENDIVE, FIG AND WALNUT SALAD

2/3 cup chopped walnuts

1/3 cup walnut oil

2 Belgian endives, leaves separated

2 cups small sprouts, such as alfalfa or radish

4 fresh figs, thinly sliced crosswise

2 scallions, thinly sliced

2 tablespoons balsamic vinegar

salt and freshly ground black pepper to taste

Serves 4
Preparation time: 15 minutes

Toss the walnuts with 1 tablespoon of the walnut oil and sauté in a skillet over medium heat for about 5 minutes, until lightly toasted. Remove with a slotted spoon to paper towels to drain. Reserve any oil in the pan.

Arrange the endive leaves on 4 serving plates. Top with the sprouts. Scatter the fig slices over the sprouts. Top with the scallions and walnuts.

In a small bowl, combine the vinegar with the salt and pepper to taste. Add the walnut oil in the skillet to the remaining walnut oil and, while whisking, add it to the small bowl in a thin stream. Adjust seasoning to taste and drizzle over the salads. Serve at once.

MUSHROOM SALAD WITH PARMESAN AND PINE NUTS

1 garlic clove, crushed

$1/2$ pound mushrooms, stems trimmed flush with caps, caps thinly sliced

$1/4$ cup extra-virgin olive oil

$1/2$ cup pine nuts

2 tablespoons fresh lemon juice

1 tablespoon chopped fresh oregano (or $1^1/2$ teaspoons dried)

salt and freshly ground black pepper to taste

3 ounces fresh young Parmesan cheese
red leaf lettuce leaves (optional)

Rub the inside of a salad bowl with the garlic clove. Discard the garlic. Add the sliced mushrooms to the bowl.

In a small skillet, heat the olive oil over medium heat. Add the pine nuts and sauté until golden brown, about 2 to 3 minutes. Dump the nuts and oil into the salad bowl and toss to coat.

Add the lemon juice, oregano, salt and pepper. Toss thoroughly but gently for about 2 minutes. (The salad can be assembled to this point and refrigerated.) Using a vegetable peeler, shave paper-thin slices of Parmesan and break them into 1-inch pieces. Add them to the bowl, tossing gently to combine. Serve in the bowl or place the lettuce leaves on salad plates and mound the salad on the leaves.

Serves 4
Preparation time: 20 minutes

SMOKED CHICKEN, PINEAPPLE AND MACADAMIA SALAD

1¹/₂ pounds boneless smoked chicken, cut into ¹/₂-inch dice

1¹/₂ cups thinly sliced celery

1 medium-size fresh pineapple, peeled,cored and cut into bite-size pieces

²/₃ cup mayonnaise, preferably homemade

1¹/₂ teaspoons Dijon mustard 2 tablespoons raspberry or sherry vinegar

salt and freshly ground black pepper to taste

1 cup coarsely chopped roasted macadamia nuts

celery leaves for garnish

Serves 6

Preparation time: 5 minutes

In a salad or mixing bowl, combine the chicken, celery and pineapple.

In a small bowl, combine the remaining ingredients except the macadamia nuts and celery leaves. Toss with the ingredients in the larger bowl. Refrigerate until serving time.

Garnish with the nuts and celery leaves before serving.

WILD RICE SALAD WITH APRICOTS AND PECANS

1 cup wild rice

³/₄ cup moist dried apricots, thinly sliced

1 cup fresh orange juice

³/₄ teaspoon salt

2 teaspoons fresh lemon juice

1 tablespoon minced shallot

salt and freshly ground black pepper to taste

¹/₃ cup extra-virgin olive oil

¹/₄ cup finely chopped parsley

1 cup coarsely chopped roasted pecans

Rinse the rice, cover it with cold water and let it soak for 30 minutes.

Place the sliced apricots in a small bowl and pour the orange juice over them. Set aside.

Drain the rice. Bring one quart of water to a boil in a medium-size saucepan. Add the salt and rice and return the water to a boil. Cover, lower the heat and simmer until the rice is tender but chewy about 30 minutes. Drain the rice. Drain the apricots, reserving the juice, and add the apricots to the rice. Toss to combine.

In a small bowl, whisk 5 tablespoons of the reserved orange juice with the lemon juice, shallot, salt and pepper. Whisk in the olive oil and toss the rice mixture with this dressing. Add the parsley and pecans and toss to combine thoroughly. Serve at room temperature.

Serves 6

Preparation time: 1 hour 10 minutes

CHESTNUT, DATE AND APPLE SALAD

1 pound chestnuts, shelled and peeled

3 cups chicken broth

1 bay leaf

$^1/_2$ pound pitted dates, halved

1 large red-skinned apple

1 large green-skinned apple

1 medium-size carrot, scraped and thinly sliced

3 scallions, sliced diagonally

1 garlic clove, minced

2 tablespoons fresh lemon juice

1$^1/_2$ teaspoons curry powder

salt and freshly ground black pepper to taste

$^1/_3$ cup olive oil

Place the chestnuts in a small saucepan with the broth and bay leaf. Bring to a simmer, cover and continue to simmer for 30 to 40 minutes or until the chestnuts are tender. Keep the heat low so the chestnuts don't fall apart. Allow them to cool in the cooking liquid. (Cooling can be hastened by setting the pan in a sink filled with 1 or 2 inches of cold water.)

Drain the chestnuts and remove the bay leaf.

In a salad or mixing bowl, combine the chestnuts and dates. Without peeling, quarter, core and slice the apples and add them to the bowl along with the carrot and scallions.

In a small bowl, whisk together the garlic, lemon juice, curry powder, salt and pepper. Whisk in the olive oil and toss with the salad ingredients. Serve at once.

Serves 6

Preparation time: 1 hour

SHRIMP SALAD WITH CASHEWS

1 pound large raw shrimp, shelled and deveined

$^1/_4$ cup peanut or vegetable oil

1 teaspoon cayenne pepper

3 scallions, sliced diagonally

1 large red-skinned apple

$^1/_4$ cup fresh lime juice

$^1/_3$ cup loosely packed fresh mint leaves

$^2/_3$ cup roasted cashews

red leaf lettuce leaves

Place the shrimp in a bowl and toss with 1 tablespoon of the oil and the cayenne pepper. Grill the shrimp over hot coals or under a broiler, about 2 to 3 minutes per side, until they are firm and pink. (Placing the shrimp on bamboo skewers will make them easier to handle.) Place the grilled shrimp in a bowl (removing them from the skewers if used). Add the scallions. Without peeling the apple, quarter and core it, then thinly slice it. Add it to the bowl. Combine the remaining oil with the lime juice and pour over the salad ingredients. Toss thoroughly to coat. Add the mint leaves and cashews and toss again. Serve on the lettuce leaves.

Serves 4 to 6

Preparation time: 15 minutes

MIXED GREEN SALAD WITH BRAZIL NUTS

1 large egg

1 garlic clove, crushed

$^1/_2$ teaspoon salt

3 tablespoons fresh lemon juice

1 teaspoon dry mustard

$^1/_4$ teaspoon Worcestershire sauce

1 tablespoon grated Parmesan cheese

freshly ground black pepper to taste

$^1/_2$ cup extra-virgin olive oil

$^3/_4$ cup shelled and sliced Brazil nuts

1 pound mixed salad greens (romaine, Boston, chicory, curly endive, arugula, iceberg, watercress, mizumi, spinach, mustard, etc.), washed thoroughly, dried and torn into bite-size pieces, about 6 to 8 cups

Serves 4 to 6
Preparation time: 25 minutes

Slip the egg into a pot of boiling water for 1 minute. Remove and set aside.

In a salad or mixing bowl, mash together the garlic clove and salt with a fork until they are well puréed. Add the lemon juice, dry mustard, Worcestershire sauce, Parmesan, pepper and egg. Whisk thoroughly

Heat the olive oil in a medium-size skillet over medium-high heat, then add the Brazil nuts. Sauté them until they are golden brown, about 2 to 3 minutes. Remove the skillet from the heat, remove the nuts with a slotted spoon and drain them on a paper towel. Don't worry about any small pieces.

Whisk the dressing mixture again while adding the hot olive oil in a stream. Add the greens to the bowl and toss thoroughly. Sprinkle with the reserved nuts, toss and serve.

CELERIAC AND HAZELNUT SLAW

3 tablespoons fresh lemon juice

1 tablespoon granulated sugar

1 pound celeriac or celery root (about 3¼ inches in diameter)

1 small red-skinned apple

1 small carrot, scraped and shredded

½ cup sour cream or plain yogurt

2 tablespoons prepared mustard

¼ cup hazelnut or olive oil

salt and freshly ground black pepper to taste

⅔ cup chopped roasted hazelnuts

Serves 6 to 8

Preparation time: 15 minutes, plus at least 2 hours to chill and 30 minutes at room temperature

In a mixing bowl, combine the lemon juice and sugar and stir until the sugar is dissolved.

Working quickly to prevent discoloration, peel the celeriac with a paring knife or nonswivelling vegetable peeler. (You won't be able to get every bit of peel out of every crack.) Using a food processor or hand grater, shred the celeriac and immediately toss with the sweetened lemon juice.

Without peeling it, core and shred the apple the same way. Then toss it with the celeriac. Add the carrot and toss to combine. In a small bowl, combine the sour cream or yogurt, mustard, oil, salt and pepper and whisk until smooth. Toss with the slaw ingredients, then cover and refrigerate for a couple of hours or overnight. Remove from the refrigerator 30 minutes before serving and sprinkle with the chopped hazelnuts.

FIVE
DESSERTS

PINE NUT SHORTBREAD

1 cup unsalted butter at room temperature

$^1/_2$ cup firmly packed light brown sugar

2 cups unbleached all-purpose flour

pinch of salt

$^3/_4$ cup pine nuts

Makes 2 dozen pieces
Preparation time: 1 hour 30 minutes

Preheat the oven to 325º.

In a large mixing bowl, cream together the butter and brown sugar until smooth, making sure no lumps of sugar remain. Add the flour and salt and work them together until a smooth dough is formed.

Place a 12- x 15-inch piece of wax paper on a cookie sheet and lightly flour it. With floured fingers, transfer the dough to the paper and pat it into a 9- x 12-inch rectangle. Scatter the pine nuts evenly over the surface and press them lightly into the dough so that the nuts are anchored. (Move any loose nuts around to open spaces.)

Cover the dough with plastic wrap or wax paper and refrigerate for 30 to 45 minutes, until hardened. Uncover the dough and slide it, along with the underlying wax paper, onto a counter. With a sharp knife or pizza cutter, cut the dough into $1^1/_2$-inch-wide strips and then into 4-inch lengths.

Place the strips $1^1/_2$ inches apart on a baking sheet and bake for 25 to 30 minutes or until delicately browned. Cool the shortbread on the baking sheet for 5 minutes, then use a spatula to remove it to racks to cool completely. Store in an airtight container.

BUTTERSCOTCH AND MACADAMIA BARS

1 cup unbleached all-purpose flour

$^1/_3$ cup confectioners' sugar

$1^1/_2$ cup unsalted butter at room temperature

6 tablespoons unsalted butter, melted

$^1/_2$ cup firmly packed dark brown sugar

1 teaspoon vanilla extract

1 large egg

2 cups roasted macadamia nuts

Makes 16 bars
Preparation time: 1 hour

Preheat the oven to 350º. Grease an 8-inch square pan.

Sift the flour and confectioners' sugar together into a small bowl. With a pastry blender, 2 knives or floured fingers, blend in the $^1/_2$ cup of butter until the mixture looks like small crumbs. Pat this mixture into the bottom of the greased pan to form a crust.

Bake the crust for 17 to 20 minutes, until lightly browned at the edges. Remove it from the oven and set it on a wire rack.

Whisk together the melted butter, brown sugar and vanilla extract until no lumps remain. Whisk in the egg and beat until the mixture resembles pudding. Add the macadamias, stirring to coat thoroughly. Pour the mixture over the crust and spread out evenly. Bake for approximately 25 minutes, until browned all over and puffed slightly in the center. Cool completely before cutting with a sharp knife into 2-inch squares.

BRAZIL NUT TORTE WITH CHOCOLATE GANACHE

2 cups shelled Brazil nuts

2 tablespoons cornstarch

1 cup granulated sugar

$^1/_4$ teaspoon salt

6 large eggs at room temperature, separated

$^1/_4$ teaspoon cream of tartar

12 shelled Brazil nuts for garnish (optional)

Chocolate Ganache:

$^1/_2$ pound semisweet chocolate

2 cups heavy cream

1 teaspoon vanilla extract

Serves 12

Preparation time: 2 hours 30 minutes

Preheat the oven to 350°.

Grease 3 8-inch round cake pans. Cut wax paper rounds to fit the bottoms of the pans. Put them in and grease them as well.

Place the Brazil nuts and cornstarch in the bowl of a blender or food processor fitted with a steel blade and process, pulsing on and off, until the mixture resembles bread crumbs. Add the sugar and salt and continue to process until well combined.

In a large mixing bowl, beat the egg yolks until frothy. Add the ground nut mixture and stir together until well combined. Set aside.

Beat the egg whites until frothy. Add the cream of tartar and continue beating until the mixture holds stiff peaks. Fold $^1/_3$ of the egg whites into the nut and egg yolk mixture until well combined. Gently fold in the remaining egg whites until thoroughly combined.

Divide the batter equally among the 3 cake pans. Bake for 25 to 30 minutes, until the cakes are golden brown and spring back in the center when touched. Remove the cakes from the oven and cool for 15 minutes. Run a sharp knife around the edge of each pan. Turn the cakes onto racks and let them cool completely. Peel off the wax paper. Meanwhile, in the top of a double boiler, combine the chocolate and $^1/_3$ cup of the cream. Heat over simmering water, stirring frequently, until the chocolate is almost melted. Remove from the heat and stir constantly until the chocolate is completely melted. Stir in vanilla extract and set aside and allow to cool to room temperature.

Chill a mixing bowl, a beater and the cream until the chocolate is at room temperature.

Beat the remaining cream until beater marks begin to show. Add the chocolate mixture and continue to beat until soft peaks form when the beaters are raised.

Spread the ganache between the layers of the cake, around the sides, and the top. Garnish the cake with whole nuts if desired.

Bittersweet Chocolate Tart with Peanut Crust

³/₄ cup roasted shelled peanuts

1¹/₄ cups unbleached all-purpose flour

¹/₄ cup granulated sugar

¹/₄ teaspoon salt

11 tablespoons unsalted butter

3 tablespoons cold water

4 large eggs

³/₄ pound bittersweet or semisweet chocolate

whipped cream (optional)

chopped roasted peanuts for garnish (optional)

Serves 6 to 8

Preparation time: 1 hour 30 minutes

Place the ³/₄ cup peanuts, flour, sugar, salt and 3 tablespoons of the butter in the bowl of a food processor fitted with a steel blade and process, pulsing on and off, until the mixture resembles coarse meal. With the motor still running, add the cold water all at once and continue processing until the mixture forms a ball or clumps together. (If it does not do so within 20 to 30 seconds, add another teaspoon of water.)

Remove the dough, dust with flour, wrap in wax paper and chill for 30 minutes.

Preheat the oven to 425°.

On a floured board or pastry cloth. roll out the dough to fit a 9-inch pie pan. (If the dough breaks or separates, just tear off a piece from the outer edge and press it into the crack.) Fold the dough in half and carefully lift into the pie pan. Unfold and press it into the pan. Cut off the overhang ¹/₂ inch from the edge of the pan. Use the scraps to repair any holes. (Dampen the scraps slightly if you have trouble getting them to stay in place.) Fold the ¹/₂-inch overhang under the edge of the pan and crimp.

Prick the dough all over with a fork and cover the crimped edges with foil strips to prevent browning. Bake in the bottom third of the oven for 10 minutes. Crack 1 egg, separating and reserving the yolk, and brush the crust with the egg white. Bake for 3 minutes more. Remove and cool on a wire rack. Remove the foil strips.

Lower the oven temperature to 350°. Put enough water in a double boiler just to reach the top section when inserted. Place the remaining butter, cut into tablespoon-size pieces, and the chocolate, broken or cut into pieces, into the top of the double boiler. Bring the water to a boil over medium-high heat. When the water begins to boil, turn off the heat, cover the pan and leave it on the stove for 10 minutes.

Uncover the pan and whisk the chocolate mixture until smooth. Remove the top part of the double boiler and set aside until just warm to the touch. Whisk in the eggs, including the reserved yolk, one at a time, beating well after each addition. Set aside.

Fill the baked crust with the chocolate mixture and bake for 20 to 25 minutes, until the filling is set and the crust is brown. Cool on a wire rack. Serve cold with whipped cream and chopped peanuts if desired, or refrigerate.

ALMOND SORBET

1 cup sliced or chopped blanched almonds

$^1/_2$ cup granulated sugar

2 cups water

$1^1/_4$ teaspoons unflavored gelatin

$^1/_3$ cup light corn syrup

$^1/_2$ teaspoon almond extract

1 tablespoon fresh lemon juice

Makes approximately 3 cups

Preparation time: 20 minutes, plus several hours to freeze

In a blender or food processor fitted with a steel blade, grind the almonds with the sugar to a fine powder.

Bring 1 cup of the water to a boil in a small saucepan. Remove the pan from the heat. Add $^1/_2$ cup of the boiling water to the almond powder and set aside for 10 minutes.

Process again, gradually adding the other $^1/_2$ cup hot water.

Sprinkle the gelatin over the remaining cup of water in a small saucepan and set aside for 3 minutes to soften. Heat over low heat, stirring occasionally, until the gelatin granules are completely dissolved. Remove from the heat and stir in the corn syrup, almond extract and lemon juice. Stir to combine. Add to the almond mixture.

Freeze in an ice cream maker according to the manufacturer's instructions or pour into ice cube trays and freeze. For the second method, early on the day of serving or even a day ahead, place half the frozen cubes in a blender or food processor fitted with a steel blade and process, pulsing on and off, until the cubes are broken and the mixture is smooth and creamy.

Pour the sorbet into a freezer-safe container. Repeat with the other cubes. Seal airtight and freeze until ready to serve.

COCONUT ICE CREAM

$^2/_3$ cup granulated sugar

4 large egg yolks

2 cups coconut milk made using all milk

$^3/_4$ cup grated fresh coconut

1 tablespoon fresh lemon juice

1 cup heavy cream

Makes 1 quart

Preparation time: 35 minutes, plus several hours to chill and freeze

In the top of a double boiler over gently boiling water, combine the sugar and egg yolks and whisk vigorously for 2 minutes. Whisk in the coconut milk and grated coconut and reduce the heat to medium. Cook the mixture, stirring constantly, for 8 to 10 minutes, until thickened slightly. Cool to room temperature. (Cooling can be hastened by pouring the mixture into a stainless-steel bowl and placing the bowl in a sink filled with 1 or 2 inches of cold water.)

Stir in the lemon juice, then the cream. Refrigerate until cold. Freeze in an ice cream freezer according to the manufacturer's instructions. Or freeze in ice-cube trays, processing in batches in food processor until smooth.

ESPRESSO AND HAZELNUT CHEESECAKE

2 cups shelled, roasted and peeled hazelnuts

$^1\!/_2$ cup unbleached all-purpose flour

$1^1\!/_4$ cups granulated sugar

3 tablespoons unsalted butter, melted

2 pounds cream cheese at room temperature

4 large eggs at room temperature

$^1\!/_4$ cup Frangelico liqueur

$^1\!/_4$ cup instant espresso powder

1 cup heavy cream at room temperature

whole roasted hazelnuts for garnish (optional)

Serves 10 to 12

Preparation time: 2 hours, plus several hours to chill and 1 hour at room temperature

Preheat the oven to 350º. Generously grease a 9-inch springform pan. Set it in the center of a 12-inch square of aluminum foil and fold up the sides. Set aside. Place the hazelnuts, flour and $^1\!/_4$ cup of the granulated sugar in a blender or food processor fitted with a steel blade. Process, pulsing on and off, until the mixture resembles bread crumbs. Place the mixture in a small bowl, add the melted butter and mix until evenly moistened. Press the mixture into the bottom and halfway up the sides of the prepared pan. Bake for 10 minutes. Let cool to room temperature.

Meanwhile, in the large bowl of an electric mixer or by hand, beat the cream cheese at low speed until soft. Add the remaining cup of sugar and beat on medium speed until light and fluffy. Add the eggs, one at a time, beating well after each addition.

In a small bowl, combine the Frangelico and espresso powder. Stir to dissolve the powder. Add to the cheese mixture along with the cream. Beat until thoroughly combined.

Pour the cheese mixture into the cooled crust. Bake for 55 minutes, turn off the oven and let the cake sit undisturbed for 45 minutes more.

Remove the pan from the oven and allow the cake to cool completely. Refrigerate for several hours or overnight. Remove from the refrigerator at least an hour before serving. Garnish with whole hazelnuts if desired.

RASPBERRY-CASHEW CRISP

1 quart raspberries

$^1/_2$ cup granulated sugar

1 tablespoon fresh lemon juice

$^1/_4$ cup dry white wine

2 tablespoons raspberry liqueur, such as Framboise or Chambord

1 cup unbleached all-purpose flour

$^1/_2$ cup firmly packed light brown sugar

6 tablespoons unsalted butter

1 cup coarsely chopped roasted cashews

whipped cream or ice cream (optional)

Serves 4 to 6

Preparation time: 1 hour

Preheat the oven to 350º.

Spread the raspberries evenly in the bottom of an 8-inch square pan and sprinkle them with the sugar. Combine the lemon juice, white wine and liqueur and drizzle evenly over the berries.

In a small bowl, combine the flour and brown sugar. Cut in the butter with a pastry blender, 2 knives or your fingers until the mixture resembles bread crumbs. Mix in the cashews and sprinkle the mixture over the raspberries.

Bake for 35 minutes or until lightly browned and bubbly. Cool for 10 to 15 minutes, serving while still warm, as is or with whipped cream or ice cream.

WHITE CHOCOLATE-PISTACHIO FUDGE

2 cups granulated sugar

³/₄ cup condensed milk

2 tablespoons fresh lemon juice

¹/₄ teaspoon salt

10 ounces good-quality white chocolate containing cocoa butter, chopped

1 teaspoon vanilla extract

1 cup shelled, peeled and roasted pistachios

Makes 36 squares
Preparation time: 1 hour 30 minutes

Butter an 8-inch square baking pan. Combine the sugar, milk, lemon juice and salt in a heavy 2-quart saucepan. Place over medium-high heat and bring to a boil, stirring frequently. When the sugar has dissolved, reduce the heat to low and cook without stirring for about 20 to 30 minutes, until a candy thermometer reads 236° or a small amount of the mixture dropped into cold water forms a soft ball. (Be sure to keep the heat on low, or the mixture will darken.) Remove the saucepan from the heat. If any sugar crystals have formed on the sides of the pan, wipe them out with a moistened pastry brush. Add the white chocolate to the pan, but do not stir. Press the chocolate down lightly into the mixture. Allow the mixture to cool to 110° or until the pan feels lukewarm to the touch. Then add the vanilla extract and beat with a wooden spoon until the mixture is thickened and smooth and has lost its sheen. (It will be quite difficult to beat the mixture, but don't stop too soon.)

Fold in the nuts and immediately scrape the fudge into the prepared pan or onto the prepared surface and spread evenly. Cool completely. Then, using a sharp knife, cut the fudge into 36 pieces about 1¹/₃ inch square. For very smooth, sharp cuts, cool the fudge in the refrigerator for 30 minutes before cutting. Store the fudge in an airtight container and serve at room temperature.

CHOCOLATE-CHESTNUT TRIFLE

1 10- or 12-ounce pound cake, thawed if frozen

¹/₃ cup seedless raspberry jam

1 cup broken chocolate wafers or cookies

1 cup marsala or cream sherry

1 cup granulated sugar

1¹/₄ cups water

1¹/₂ pounds chestnuts, shelled and peeled

2¹/₂ teaspoons vanilla extract

9 ounces semisweet chocolate

1 cup milk

pinch of salt

3 large egg yolks

2 cups heavy cream, well chilled

¹/₃ cup confectioners' sugar

glacéed cherries for garnish (optional)

Serves 8 to 10

Preparation time: 2 hours, plus several hours to set and chill

Early on the day of serving, or 1 or 2 days before, slice the pound cake into ¹/₄-inch slices and make sandwiches with the raspberry jam. Cut the sandwiches into 1-inch squares and place them in the bottom of a 3-quart glass bowl. Sprinkle the broken wafers over them and douse evenly with the marsala or sherry. Cover and refrigerate.

Chill a mixing bowl and beaters. Place the granulated sugar in a 1-quart saucepan with the water. Bring to a boil and boil for 5 minutes. Add the prepared chestnuts and 1 teaspoon of the vanilla extract and return to a boil. Lower the heat to a high simmer and cook, stirring often but gently for 15 to 20 minutes or until the chestnuts are tender. (Add a little more water if the chestnuts seem to be getting too dry). Remove from the heat and select 12 whole or nearly whole chestnuts from the pan; set them on wax paper or plastic wrap to cool. Reserve. Cool the contents of the pan completely (placing the pan in a sink filled with 1 to 2 inches of cold water will speed cooling) and then spoon the chestnuts over the chilled cookie and cake mixture. Cover and refrigerate.

Finely chop ¹/₃ pound of the chocolate and reserve. In a 1-quart saucepan over medium-high heat, bring the milk to the verge of boiling, stirring frequently. Add the chopped chocolate and salt and whisk until the chocolate is completely melted and the mixture is smooth and on the verge of boiling. Remove from the heat.

In a medium-size bowl, whisk the egg yolks briefly then, while whisking constantly pour the chocolate mixture gradually into the yolks. Add ³/₄ teaspoon of the remaining vanilla extract. Cool to room temperature (placing the bowl in a sink filled with 1 or 2 inches of cold water will hasten cooling), then pour over the chestnuts in the bowl. Cover and refrigerate until set, about 30 to 45 minutes.

In the chilled bowl, using the chilled beaters, whip the cream until it forms soft peaks. Add the confectioners' sugar and the remaining ³/₄ teaspoon vanilla extract and continue beating until stiff peaks form when the beaters are raised. Spoon or pipe the whipped cream over the chocolate custard.

Shave the remaining ounce of chocolate with a sharp knife or grater and sprinkle it over the top of the whipped cream. Arrange the reserved whole chestnuts and the glacéed cherries, if desired, on top of the whipped cream and grated chocolate. Refrigerate for several hours or overnight.

This dish may be made 1 or 2 days in advance or over 2 to 3 days. When serving, spoon all the way through the layers for each portion.

PINE NUT

Mushroom Salad with
Parmesan and Pine Nuts
88

Basil and Sun-Dried Tomato
Pesto with Walnuts and Pine
Nuts
78

Orzo with Pancetta and Pine
Nuts
54

Pine Nut Shortbread
104

PISTACHIO

Chicken Liver and Pistachio
Pâté
22

Date and Pistachio Scones
42

Scallops with Lemon and
Pistachios
68

White Chocolate-Pistachio
Fudge
116

WALNUT

Endive, Fig and Walnut Salad
86

Fried Walnut Polenta with
Gorgonzola Sauce
30

Basil and Sun-Dried Tomato
Pesto with Walnuts and Pine
Nuts
78

Turkey with Walnut Mole
Sauce
72

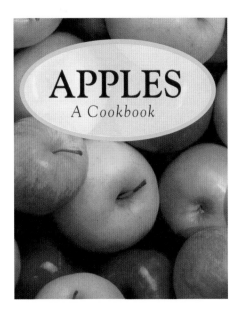

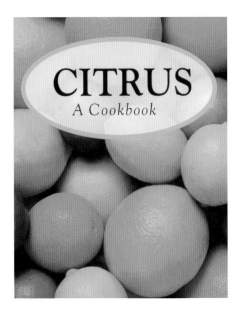

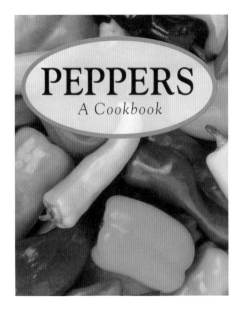